LIVING TOGETHER

EDGAR BOWERS

Living Together

NEW AND SELECTED POEMS

DAVID R. GODINE

David R. Godine Publisher
Boston, Massachusetts

LCC 73-81061
ISBN 0-87923-075-4

Of the new poems, 'Living Together' was first published in the *Denver Quarterly* and 'Wandering' in the *Southern Review*.

CONTENTS

THE FORM OF LOSS

To the Reader 9
The Wise Men 10
Oedipus at Colonus 11
Epigram on the Passing of Christmas 12
Late Winter Night 13
To Accompany an Italian Guide-book 14
Grove and Building 18
For W.A. Mozart 19
Dedication for a House 20
The Stoic: for Laura von Courten 21
Venus 23
The Snow Man 24
Amor vincit omnia 25
Two Poems on the Catholic Bavarians 26
The Virgin Considered as a Picture 28
The Prince 29
Aix-la-Chappelle 32
The Mountain Cemetery 33
From J. Haydn to Constanze Mozart (1791) 34
Dark Earth and Summer 35
Elegy: for W.C.S.H. 36
The Virgin Mary 38
Clairvoyant 39
Variations on an Elizabethan Theme 40
From William Tyndale to John Frith 41
To This Book 43

THE ASTRONOMERS

The Astronomers of Mont Blanc 47
Adam's Song to Heaven 48
An Afternoon at the Beach 49
Of an Etching 50
To Death 51
To the Contemporary Muse 52
In a Darkness 53
In the Last Circle 54
The Mirror 55
After Leconte de Lisle 56
An Answer 57
A Song for Rising 58
The Dream 59
The Centaur Overheard 60
Autumn Shade 61

NEW POEMS

Living Together 75
Wandering 76
Insomnia 81
Chorus for the Untenured Personnel 82
The Philosophical Life 83
The Elegy 84

THE FORM OF LOSS

TO THE READER

These poems are too much tangled with the error
And waste they would complete. My soul repays me,
Who fix it by a rhythm, with reason's terror
Of hearing the swift motion that betrays me.
Mine be the life and failure. But do not look
Too closely for these ghosts which claim my book.

THE WISE MEN

Far to the east I see them in my mind
Coming in every year to that one place.
They carry in their hands what they must find,
In their own faces bare what they shall face.

They move in silence, permanent and sure,
Like figurines of porcelain set with gold,
The colors of their garments bright and pure,
Their graceful features elegant and old.

They do not change; nor war nor peace define
Nor end the journey that each year the same
Renders them thus. They wait upon a sign
That promises no future but their name.

OEDIPUS AT COLONUS

Subdued essential ripened through excess,
Firm in erratic shade and dense with trial
Of who and what it is, the intellect
Measures archaic, fugitive defect,
The blind cost and compulsion, meaningless.

All given to darkness: the gulls' straying cry
Harsh over muffled sea-waste and the brine
Seething the air, incessantly may steep
The sense replacing what he could not keep,
Quickened by light and form that it put by.

Now at the last he lies back, still unspent,
In passion and in time, relinquishing
All that he gathered from them to their use,
Clasps in the dark will he could not refuse
Ingenuous patience eager with assent.

EPIGRAM ON THE PASSING OF CHRISTMAS

This is the freezing guilt I shall remember
That I would mourn for Him I do not know:
As if the loss of some life-giving member
Had doomed Him as a seasonal man of snow.

LATE WINTER NIGHT

From darkness in the other room, I hear
A labored breathing, which disease decays,
By one who cannot add another year
To twenty-five, whose gentle mind delays,
By lonely force of will, its certain end.

I have been reading and will read again,
Except a sudden grieving interrupt,
The work of them who claim life brooks no pain
Unless we have desires it may corrupt;
And therefore of desire desire an end.

If I might read all night, all the next day,
Read without food or sleep, not think or see,
Such old chimeras might not then display
So little comment on finality,
Nor life seem more than beginning brought to end.

But while he sleeps, I call again to mind
Persons and places, all the life we know,
And, once more, try to realize, half blind,
The stunning agony of being slow
To choose the certain meaning in the end,

Which will abide when such as we are lost
And places changed. Despite this brief, dark age,
Who dares to take his living at no cost?
We rather lose it all, lest patient rage
Be put aside before it, too, must end.

TO ACCOMPANY AN ITALIAN GUIDE-BOOK

1

Beside the Adriatic a strand lies
Cut off from tidal violence by shoals
And low dunes tufted with sparse grass, where gulls
Repeat the air and water in their cries.

A tourist once might find at dusk that place,
Seeking a chapel, rumored to have stood
Neglected by the years, and past driftwood
Approach the curve of ruined beach, to trace,

Upon his knees, a dead gull's form, blue-white
And shrunk in sand; or rescue from debris
A conch from whose bright curving rooms the sea
Mounts subtler through his ear than through his sight;

Or while the darkness washes what he sees,
Come down behind the tide to a pool, blue
As deep sea water and as still, to view
Red coral arms, azure anemones,

And living shells which, secret and intense,
Add curve on curve of marble surfaced lime
To their perfection, while the whole of time
Seems brought to bear on underwater silence.

2

The equinoctial rains began toward dawn
And would have drenched his pillow, had he not
Been wakened by their sudden coming on
In time to pull his double windows shut.

The down-pour struck the water into foam
Below the casement, and the off-sea squall
Blew chill against his face. The heavy gloom
Concealed without a break the Grand Canal,

Where earlier in the evening through the heat
Gondolas came from Lido, black prows high
And lamps reflecting orange streaks on wet,
To land where Stephen dominates the sky.

There, though the outside wash against the glass
Obscured the stone in which great works decay,
He contemplated in its shifting mass
The dense and shadowy basilica

Of Saint Mark floating on the Square, as when
The Slavic fleet crept toward it from the sea
With muffled oars, concealed by mist and rain
And early morning darkness, silently,

Past Arsenal and *dromi* anchored near,
Feeding their pirate cunning on the rich
Shadow of treasure glimmering in the air,
And waiting for the drag of hull on beach.

3

A chalk white road bends dusty through plane trees
And gleams past tawny fields, mown yesterday,
Where now and then late gleaners quit the shade
To gather what remains there of the hay.

Up foothills by stripped orchards, sweet with fruit
That fell before the picking underfoot,
Ferment for bees, and vineyards where of late
Full clusters hung down purple to the root,

It gains a meadow overlooking valleys
And narrow rivers on whose flow the leaves
Go touched with fiery coolness to the sea.
The meadow's edge is piled around with sheaves,

And near them on smooth grass the harvesters
Assemble in a row to celebrate
The season, as lost generations did
Upon that spot at this same lunar date.

Together with fine movements they inherit
They purify of accidental dross
Each gesture, simple as the body is
But more complex with living and its loss,

To verify their being by their doing;
While in the woods and thickets, savage chromes
Lose, destitute of birds, their summer shapes,
And bees grow numb about their sated combs.

4

Beneath the fronds of palms, pale succulents,
Small oaks with leaves like ilex leaves, and cactus,
Whose ivory pallor does not seem to live,
A hermit worshipped secret, fugitive,
Sweet gods of his more youthful innocence.

He rose, as soon as little night-birds shook
Themselves awake and stirred like ilex leaves
Along the quiet limbs of the oak trees,
To bring new honey, milk, and fruit to these
Shy transients of the stream, trunk, mist, and rock.

Lo, in the half-light, coming, anxiously
Child-like and tender, Etruscan, German, Greek,
Familiar exiles, delicate surprise
Trembling on little feet, their shining eyes
Alert mid foliage parted cautiously;

Rapid as moon-ray on the darkening air
And sudden in the moon-light, satyr, faun,
Maenad and nymph, light goddess and slim god –
Leaving no print at all where they have trod
And silent as the dew-fall, they appear.

Their coming how propitious to the mind
That breathlessly gentle as the warm eye-lid
Would echo softly the soft-running blood,
Yet would, exact, trace of beatitude
The tenderness less easily defined,

The tenderness the hermit might increase
If, turning from among the simply fed,
He fed his spirit, disciplined and good,
On the fierce knowledge innocence withstood
Of Christ and of compulsion that will cease.

GROVE AND BUILDING

'Au soleil, dans l'immense forme du ciel pur ...'
– Paul Valéry

When, having watched for a long time the trees
Scatter the sun among their shaded places,
You turn away, your face is many faces,
Each formed by the resistance of the leaves.

And through the dim contagion in your eyes
The agony of light which shade refuses
With bright decay a near facade infuses,
Drenched by the ebbing warmth of Paradise.

Its granite vaults the reach of passive trees,
And, shadowless, its final line of being
Extends a line beyond your shaded seeing
To train your sight on nothing that it sees.

There, at that moment of arrest, you feel
Against the blood veiling the eyes' repose
The prudent sun, the blood red solar Rose,
Unshadowed being turning like a wheel

At once clock-wise and also counter-wise;
Thus from its light whose motion is unending
All shadows turn and, on one axis bending,
Lose their umbrageous choice within your eyes.

FOR W.A. MOZART

Against each perfect note I bear all thought.
Before the passion of thy complex grace
Flesh melts from bone that lies across the face,
And thought lies bare to what thy genius wrought.

But thought to most with faint acceptance blames,
Who find no human feeling in such form;
And the desire that rhetoric perform
Its unique cries I counter with no claims

But say that in Saalfelden once I played
Upon thine own clavier, now black with age,
Some remnant of thy sweet and decorous rage
Until such condescending minds, afraid
To cant against such naked elegance,
Could speak no more of spectacular innocence.

DEDICATION FOR A HOUSE

We, who were long together homeless, raise
Brick walls, wood floors, a roof, and windows up
To what sustained us in those threatening days
Unto this end. Alas, that this bright cup
Be empty of the care and life of him
Who should have made it overflow its brim.

THE STOIC: FOR LAURA VON COURTEN

All winter long you listened for the boom
Of distant cannon wheeled into their place.
Sometimes outside beneath a bombers' moon
You stood alone to watch the searchlights trace

Their careful webs against the boding sky,
While miles away on Munich's vacant square
The bombs lunged down with an unruly cry
Whose blast you saw yet could but faintly hear.

And might have turned your eyes upon the gleam
Of a thousand years of snow, where near the clouds
The Alps ride massive to their full extreme,
And season after season glacier crowds

The dark, persistent smudge of conifers.
Or seen beyond the hedge and through the trees
The shadowy forms of cattle on the furze,
Their dim coats white with mist against the freeze.

Or thought instead of other times than these,
Of other countries and of other sights:
Eternal Venice sinking by degrees
Into the very water that she lights;

Reflected in canals, the lucid dome
Of Maria dell'Salute at your feet,
Her triple spires disfigured by the foam.
Remembered in Berlin the parks, the neat

Footpaths and lawns, the clean spring foliage,
Where just short weeks before, a bomb, unaimed,
Released a frightened lion from its cage,
Which in the mottled dark that trees enflamed

Killed one who hurried homeward from the raid.
And by yourself there standing in the chill
You must, with so much known, have been afraid
And chosen such a mind of constant will,

Which, though all time corrode with constant hurt,
Remains, until it occupies no space,
That which it is; and passionless, inert,
Becomes at last no meaning and no place.

VENUS

Her constant gesture spanned the air,
And constant eyes befogged our eyes
Whose guilty cast and devious stare
Sought knowledge in a vain surmise.

For all about her, nature rose
In harmony with our distress,
But in her face profound repose,
A surety profounder, yes,

Than any promised us by them
Who measure life for measure's sake,
(Forgetting their own secret phlegm,
They measure error by mistake.)

With caution and with small belief
That in her posture we should find
More than she showed us, constant grief,
More than we showed her, constant mind,

We moved within her gesture's space.
Then marble grew our bones and flesh
And from the head to line the face
Came brain's entangled, mended mesh.

THE SNOW MAN

Some boys rolled up a snow man in the yard
Whose idle face I watch these lunar nights;
His lack of something makes him prey to thaw,
Dumb show of nothing, to come and go with ice.

Yet in the night I start up with the crack
Of ice upon the dormant pool and range,
From dreams of snow men melting on the grass,
Convulsed with frantic change and counter change.

He shall not be there when the summer spends
All it has brought to life; yet freeze will stir
Behind each burning day, in steaming pool
And on the dusty lawn and range, to blur,

When lunar glare is falsely spread like snow,
My sleep with images of a snow man,
Standing always in formulative cold
In what must be perfect meridian.

AMOR VINCIT OMNIA

Love is no more.
It died as the mind dies: the pure desire
Relinquishing the blissful form it wore,
The ample joy and clarity expire.

Regret is vain.
Then do not grieve for what you would efface,
The sudden failure of the past, the pain
Of its unwilling change, and the disgrace.

Leave innocence,
And modify your nature by the grief
Which poses to the will indifference
That no desire is permanent in sense.

Take leave of me.
What recompense, or pity, or deceit
Can cure, or what assumed serenity
Conceal the mortal loss which we repeat?

The mind will change, and change shall be relief.

TWO POEMS ON THE CATHOLIC BAVARIANS

1

The fierce and brooding holocaust of faith
This people conquered, which no edict could,
And wove its spirit stiff and rich like cloth
That many years ago was soaked in blood.

Their minds are active only in their hands
To check and take the labor of the hills,
To furnish nature its precise demands
And bear its harshness as it seems God wills.

But holy passion hurts them in each season
To blend themselves with nature if they can;
They find in well known change enough of reason
To worship Him in it as Him in Man.

Thus in the summer on the Alpine heights
A deity of senseless wrath and scorn
Is feasted through the equinoctial nights
As though a savage Christ were then reborn.

Up from the floors of churches in December
The passion rises to a turbulence
Of darkness such as threatens to dismember
The mind submerged in bestial innocence.

And Druid shades with old dementia fraught
Possess the souls they had accounted loss
And join their voices, raging and distraught,
About the curious symbol of the cross.

2

I know a wasted place high in the Alps
Called Witches' Kitchen. There the sun all day
With aberrant change of shadows plagues the eyes,
And when the equinoctial moon has play

Upon the beast-like monoliths of stone,
The blood runs cold as its old passions rise
To haunt the memory of what we are
And what we do in worshipping brute skies.

Below this waste of spirit and of mind
The village Holy Blood with ordered care
Was founded on deep meadows. Yearly, sheep
Are brought to graze in summer pastures there.

Its people sow and harvest grain together
Between the comings of the winter's ice,
And when they stop to take a quick sprung flower,
Its being and their gesture will suffice

To balance what they are and what are not.
And if we turn to look within the town
Upon a wall we find the stencilled group
Of Mary, John, and others taking down

The body of their Master from the tree.
And just at dusk the daylight's weakened pace
Shades the blue chalk of Mary's robe with red;
And her faint tears are red upon His face:

THE VIRGIN CONSIDERED AS A PICTURE

Her unawed face, whose pose so long assumed
Is touched with what reality we feel,
Bends to itself and, to itself resumed,
Restores a tender fiction to the real.

And in her artful posture movement lies
Whose timeless motion flesh must so conceal;
Yet what her pose conceals we might surmise
And might pretend to gather from her eyes

The final motion flesh gives up to art.
But slowly, if we watch her long enough,
The nerves grow subtler, and she moves apart

Into a space too dim with time and blood
For our set eyes to follow true enough,
Or nerves to guess about her, if they would.

THE PRINCE

I come to tell you that my son is dead.
Americans have shot him as a spy.
Our heritage has wasted what it shaped,
And he the ruin's proof. I suffered once
My self-destruction like a pleasure, gave
Over to what I could not understand
The one whom all my purpose was to save.
Deceit was the desire to be deceived,
For, when I kissed illusion's face, tears gushed
Warm under anguished eye-lids, and were dried
By new desire that chilled me like a wind –
As if it were defeat being alive
And hurt should yet restore me and be joy,
Joy without cause! Longing without an end,
That could not love the thing which it desired.
Through all that time I craved magnificence
Of the doomed fox – black paws, white throat, and red
Coat dragged among crisp yellow leaves, along
A stream trout break all night with glistening rise,
Austere, old lonely grandeur's complete pride
The pack's mute victim, while the crimson eyes
Glitter with Epicurus's innocence.
Giddy with lack of hope, my mind foresaw
Itself, still barely human and by duress
Bound in heroic trance, take glittering
Impassive armor up and crowd the niche
Of time with iron necessity; and, hard
With loss and disbelief, approved its choice.

This is the time's presumption: ignorance
Denies what we have been and might become.
So will and thought are mirrors of themselves.
Uniquely the strange object I might know,
I chose to live, who else had found no reason

In vanity's contempt, by simple faith
In what had been before me, and restored
The name of duty to a shadow, spent
Of meaning and obscure with rage and doubt
Intense as cold. My son, who was the heir
To every hope and trust, grew out of caring
Into the form of loss as I had done,
And then betrayed me who betrayed him first.
You know despair's authority, the rite
And exaltation by which we are governed,
A state absurd with wrath that we are human,
Nothing, to which our nature would submit.
Such was the German state. Yet, like a fool,
I hated it, my image, and was glad
When he refused its service; now I know
That even his imprisonment was mine,
A gesture by the will to break the will.
Honoring it, I dreamed again the fierce
Abandonment to what one hates, the fox
Sacred in pain and helplessness. O sages,
Of whom we are the merest shades, you are
The undemanding whom indifference
Has least defiled, those few whose innocence
Is earned by long distraction with minute
And slow corruption proving all they know,
Till patience, young in what may come to pass,
Is reconciled to what its love permits,
And is not proud that knowledge must be so.

By what persuasion he saw fit to change
Allegiance, none need wonder. Let there be,
However, no mistake: those who deny
What they believe is true, desire shall mock
And crime's uncertain promise shall deceive.
Alas, that he was not a German soldier
In his apostasy, but would put on
The parody of what caprice put off,
Enemy in disguise, the uniform
And speech of what the sceptic heart requires!
Ruthless the irony that is its thought.
The soldier's death should find him unaware,
The breathless air close round him as sleep falls,
Sudden with ripeness, heavy with release.
Thereby the guileless tranquilly are strong:
The man is overwhelmed, the deed remains.
Flesh of my flesh, bewildered to despair
And fallen outside the limits of my name,
Forever lies apart and meaningless.
I who remain perceive the dear, familiar
Unblemished face of possibility
Drenched by a waste profound with accident,
His childhood face concealed behind my face.
Where is the guile enough to comfort me?

AIX-LA-CHAPPELLE, 1945

How quietly in ruined state
The effigy of Charles the Great
Wastes in the rain! Baton and orb,
The rigid figure and the crown,
Tarnished by air and wet, absorb
His change, impassive in renown.

Northward along the Rhine, towns lie
Shattered by vague artillery:
Julich, Düren, whose Rathaus doors
The molten eagles seal, effaced,
Like Gladbach's partial walls and floors,
By snow impersonal as waste.

The South's white cities, terrible
With sensuous calm and beauty, fall
Through darkness to their fragrant streets.
France's smooth armor seeps her blood.
The European plain repeats
Its ageless night of ice and mud.

Despair shall rise. The dragon's gore
From off the torn cathedral floor
Forces his mind's dark cavity:
His sleep has been his innocence,
And his malignant growth shall be
Monstered by lucid violence.

THE MOUNTAIN CEMETERY

With their harsh leaves old rhododendrons fill
The crevices in grave plots' broken stones.
The bees renew the blossoms they destroy,
While in the burning air the pines rise still,
Commemorating long forgotten biers,
Whose roots replace the semblance of these bones.

The weight of cool, of imperceptible dust
That came from nothing and to nothing came
Is light within the earth and on the air.
The change that so renews itself is just.
The enormous, sundry platitude of death
Is for these bones, bees, trees, and leaves the same.

And splayed upon the ground and through the trees
The mountains' shadow fills and cools the air,
Smoothing the shape of headstones to the earth.
The rhododendrons suffer with the bees
Whose struggles loose ripe petals to the earth,
The heaviest burden it shall ever bear.

Our hard earned knowledge fits us for such sleep.
Although the spring must come, it passes too
To form the burden suffered for what comes.
Whatever we would give our souls to keep
Is only part of what we call the soul;
What we of time would threaten to undo

All time in its slow scrutiny has done.
For on the grass that starts about the feet
The body's shadow turns, to shape in time,
Soon grown preponderant with creeping shade,
The final shadow that is turn of earth;
And what seems won paid for as in defeat.

FROM J. HAYDN TO CONSTANZE MOZART (1791)

Incredibly near the vital edge of tears,
I write, Constanze, having heard our loss.
Only the shape of memory adheres
To the most nearly perfect human pose
I hope to find, though mind and heart grow fierce,
Five times again as fierce as his repose.

The mind of most of us is trivial;
The heart is moved too quickly and too much.
He thought each movement that was animal,
And senses were the mind's continual search
To find the perfect note, emotional
And mental, each the other one's reproach.

With him as master, grief should be serene,
Death its own joy, and joy opposed by death,
What is made living by what should have been,
And understanding constant in its wrath
Within one life to fix them both the same,
Though no one can, unless it be in death.

Yet we who loved him have that right to mourn.
Let this be mine, that fastened on my eyes
I carry one small memory of his form
Aslant at his clavier, with careful ease,
To bring one last enigma to the norm,
Intelligence perfecting the mute keys.

DARK EARTH AND SUMMER

Earth is dark where you rest
Though a little winter grass
Glistens in icy furrows.
There, cautious, as I pass,

Squirrels run, leaving stains
Of their nervous, minute feet
Over the tombs; and near them
Birds grey and gravely sweet.

I have come, warm of breath,
To sustain unbodied cold,
Removed from life and seeking
Darkness where flesh is old,

Flesh old and summer waxing,
Quick eye in the sunny lime,
Sweet apricots in silence
Falling – precious in time,

All radiant as a voice, deep
As their oblivion. Only as I may,
I come, remember, wait,
Ignorant in grief, yet stay.

What you are will outlast
The warm variety of risk,
Caught in the wide, implacable,
Clear gaze of the basilisk.

ELEGY: FOR W.C.S.H.

My feeling is a posture where the sun
Warms with bright change my marble sleep, while I
Discover shade, oblivion, and death
Fixed in my head behind each carnal eye,
And sink within the darkness which I am.
Knowledge is cold along the flowing nerve
Which moves the blood; touched by no will of mine,
Its masses stir through action from reserve.

The light streams as if perfect through my eyes
Which may perceive it only on the grass
Where leaves have edged bright quality with shade;
Or if I raise them, they become a mass
Of hawthorn blossoms where bees crawl and cling
Lightly in their instinctive ecstasy:
Or eyelids brush away both sun and shade,
Of which I keep but their contingency.

Though passion after life may be concealed
In a marmoreal brooding, it is stirred
And shaded by some transitory thing,
As polished walls reflect a flying bird;
And though within my flesh I move untouched
By loss outside its pale security
And selfish care, the ways of knowledge hurt
As if they were the tongues of flattery.

His nerves have left his figure loose, as mine
Must let it go, and with it memories
So violent they dominate the sense,
Lest mind should settle like soft dust in trees
Where efforts of the will might stir its faint
Invisibility from leaf to leaf,
Pale membrane over matter in the sun,
Blurred by an imprecise and feral grief.

Our wisdom's face becomes mundane repose.
The head fallen back in agony, the eyes
Beclouded and the whitened lips benumbed
Distort the grieving figure from its guise,
Until the brain, achieving what is lost,
Assumes the living stone's integrity
And fluid sameness, line by elusive line
Of bitter, phidian serenity.

THE VIRGIN MARY

The hovering and huge, dark, formless sway
That nature moves by laws we contemplate
We name for lack of name as order, fate,
God, principle, or primum mobile.
But in that graven image, word made wood
By skillful faith of him to whom she was
Eternal nature, first and final cause,
The form of knowledge knowledge understood
Bound human thought against the dark we find.
And body took the image of the mind
To shape in chaos a congruent form
Of will and matter, equal, side by side,
Upon the act of faith, within the norm
Of carnal being, blind and glorified.

CLAIRVOYANT

The full hours turn, and overhead
Far wandering fires seem candid fields;
Awash with silence, our small bed
Drifts through the order passion yields.

Some kind aspect has brought us so
To secure each other from duress
That we may help illusion grow
From promise into happiness.

Despite erratic fires which chance
In self-consuming, bright array
Hurls from our gaze, let us advance
Desire that puts despair away,

In loving keeps the hope for love,
And, though inconstant and perverse,
Conform to law in how we move
Like lucid stars; let love coerce.

Who knows what forms desire? The hand
Once ardent on your face tonight
Lies sorrowing. Yet, as nights expand
Ephemeral hours slowly to light,

So we may keep, though change dissuade,
A hope grown tranquil, candid, sure,
And these short hours desire has made
Ample and joyful, will mature

Renewal from the past, our ease
And our desire: the grave descent
Of lonely Venus offer peace,
A time prepared for ecstasies,
Profusion mild and immanent.

VARIATIONS ON AN ELIZABETHAN THEME

Long days, short nights, this Southern summer
Fixes the mind within its timeless place.
Athwart pale limbs the brazen hummer
Hangs and is gone, warm sound its quickened space.

Butterfly weed and cardinal flower,
Orange and red, with indigo the band,
Perfect themselves unto the hour.
And blood suffused within the sunlit hand,

Within the glistening eye the dew,
Are slow with their slow moving. Watch their passing,
As lightly the shade covers you:
All colors and all shapes enrich its massing.

Once I endured such gentle season.
Blood-root, trillium, sweet flag, and swamp aster –
In their mild urgency, the reason
Knew each and kept each chosen from disaster.

Now even dusk destroys; the bright
Leucothoë dissolves before the eyes
And poised upon the reach of light
Leaves only what no reasoning dare surmise.

Dim isolation holds the sense
Of being, intimate as breathing; around,
Voices, unmeasured and intense,
Throb with the heart below the edge of sound.

FROM WILLIAM TYNDALE TO JOHN FRITH*

The letters I, your lone friend, write in sorrow
Will not contain my sorrow: it is mine,
Not yours who stand for burning in my place.
Be certain of your fate. Though some, benign,
Will urge by their sweet threats malicious love
And counsel dangerous fear of violence,
Theirs is illusion's goodness proving fair –
Against your wisdom – worldly innocence
And just persuasions' old hypocrisy.
Making their choice, reflect what you become;
Horror and misery bringing ruin where
The saintly mind has treacherously gone numb;
Despair in the deceit of your remorse
As, doubly heretic, you waste your past
Recanting, by all pitied, honorless,
Until you choose more easy death at last.
Think too of me. Sometimes in morning dark
I let my candle gutter and sit here
Brooding, as shadows fill my cell and sky
Breaks pale outside my window; then the dear
Companionship we spent working for love
Compels me to achieve a double portion.
In spite of age, insanity, despair,
Grief, or declining powers, we have done
What passes to the living of all men
Beyond our weariness. The fire shall find
Me hidden here, although its pain be less
If you have gone to it with half my mind,

*John Frith, Tyndale's most loyal disciple, returned to England from the continent in 1533, when he was thirty years old. He was arrested and burned at the stake. This letter would have been written to Frith in prison from Tyndale in Holland, where, not long after, he too was imprisoned and burned at the stake for heresy.

Leaving me still enough to fasten flesh
Against the stake, flesh absolute with will.
And should your human powers and my need
Tremble at last and grow faint, worn, and ill,
Pain be too much to think of, fear destroy,
And animal reluctance from the womb,
Endurance of your end's integrity,
Be strong in this: heaven shall be your tomb.

TO THIS BOOK

Little book, you are the white flakes which fell
In several quiet winters, from a sky
Edging abandoned landscape, narrow and strange.
You are the flakes, and all the rest was I,
The sky, the landscape, and the freezing spell.

THE ASTRONOMERS

THE ASTRONOMERS OF MONT BLANC

Who are you there that, from your icy tower,
Explore the colder distances, the far
Escape of your whole universe to night;
That watch the moon's blue craters, shadowy crust,
And blunted mountains mildly drift and glare,
Ballooned in ghostly earnest on your sight;
Who are you, and what hope persuades your trust?

It is your hope that you will know the end
And compass of our ignorant restraint
There in lost time, where what was done is done
Forever as a havoc overhead.
Aging, you search to master in the faint
Persistent fortune which you gaze upon
The perfect order trusted to the dead.

ADAM'S SONG TO HEAVEN

You shall be as gods, knowing good and evil

O depth sufficient to desire,
Ghostly abyss wherein perfection hides,
Purest effect and cause, you are
The mirror and the image love provides.

All else is waste, though you reveal
Lightly upon your luminous bent shore
Color, shape, odor, weight, and voice,
Bright mocking hints that were not there before,

And all your progeny time holds
In timeless birth and death. But, when, for bliss,
Loneliness would possess its like,
Mine is the visage yours leans down to kiss.

Beautiful you are, fair deceit!
Knowledge is joy where your unseeing eyes
Shine with the tears that I have wept
To be the sum of all your thoughts devise.

Flawless you are, unlimited
By other than yourself, yet suffer pain
Of the nostalgias I have felt
For love beyond the end your eyes contain;

Then, solitary, drift, inert,
Through the abyss where you would have me go
And, lost to your desire at last,
Ravish the waste for what you cannot know.

What are you then! Delirium
Receives the image I despair to keep,
And knowledge in your somber depth
Embraces your perfection and your sleep.

AN AFTERNOON AT THE BEACH

I'll go among the dead to see my friend.
The place I leave is beautiful: the sea
Repeats the winds' far swell in its long sound,
And, there beside it, houses solemnly
Shine with the modest courage of the land,
While swimmers try the verge of what they see.

I cannot go, although I should pretend
Some final self whose phantom eye could see
Him who because he is not cannot change.
And yet the thought of going makes the sea,
The land, the swimmers, and myself seem strange,
Almost as strange as they will someday be.

OF AN ETCHING

Toward me, seated, young, spent by war, bend two,
Lover, mother, perhaps, future and past,
Memory of peace, worn tranquillity.
But I, seated on a tomb, ride the swift
Invisible wave: young, weary, estranged,
Turn toward you, gazing over my shoulder,
Forgetting. Forgetting armor's embrace,
Riding the tomb, lonely, suffering myself,
I, present forever, forever turn
Toward you, stranger, for whom I stay the same
Young man, both self and mortuary urn.

TO DEATH

If I am but the unmysterious sum
Of each event which all the past has sealed
    And I repeat,
You are the mark of that delirium
By which desire for limit is revealed,
    And for defeat
To which I understand I, too, must come.

If I can only be as I have been
And yet through timeless time and spaceless space
    Vary by chance,
You are the trust which my pretended pain
And hope and purpose form here in the grace
    Of circumstance,
The grace I cannot prove but would sustain.

Dear mercy, with your old ambiguous smile,
Meaningless life contrives your sacrifice.
    Though all event
Ignore your magnitude a little while,
Your claim is real, and must at last suffice
    All who dissent,
Our comfort, and the limit of our guile.

TO THE CONTEMPORARY MUSE

Honesty, little slut, must you insist
On hearing every dirty word I know
And all my worst affairs? Are impotence,
Insanity, and lying what you lust for?
Your hands are cold, feeling me in the dark.

IN A DARKNESS

I watch no comfort bent across the grass
Which was my shadow. Here, alone, I pass
Bereft of him whose trust I took on trust.
And, bound by neither lust nor thought of lust,
By neither warmth nor cold, stand so alone,
So exiled to some future monotone,
That should my hand grope upward to my face,
All it could touch might seem a little space.
Even its dim report might cease, somewhere
Between the ends of darkness and of air.

IN THE LAST CIRCLE

You spoke all evening hatred and contempt,
The ethical distorted to a fury
Of self-deception, malice, and conceit,
Yourself the judge, the lawyer, and the jury.
I listened, but, instead of proof, I heard,
As if the truth were merely what you knew,
Wrath cry aloud its wish and its despair
That all would be and must be false to you.

You are the irresponsible and damned,
Alone in final cold athwart your prey.
Your passion eats his brain. Compulsively,
The crime which is your reason eats away
Compassion, as they both have eaten you,
Till what you are is merely what you do.

THE MIRROR

Father, I loved you as a child, and still,
When trouble bruises him whom I retrace
Back to the time I cannot know, I fill,
By my desire, the possible with grace,
And wait your coming. Then I see my face,
Breathed by some other presence on the chill
Illumination of this mortal glass,
Gleam from the dark to struggle in your will.

In that fixed place, around me, others move,
Vivid with long conclusion, who, once dead,
Quickened the little moment I could prove;
And, though I seem to live, there, at my head,
As if the thought translating all I see,
He stands, who was my future, claiming me.

AFTER LECONTE DE LISLE

Under the dense sycamore, she sleeps,
Virginal, in a garden white and dry.
An azure butterfly
Has escaped the shade to hover at her lips.

Long the sun polishes the white sky.
While, steeped in silence, through the sleeping grapes,
The future wakes, she sleeps,
Dreams, her chaste mouth smiling as the blue light sips.

Spirit kiss possessing her rapt lips
Awakens in her cool, deep, leafy sleep
Love without human shape,
Young desire aroused to grave activity.

Revery swims! Soundless the dark sleep
It swims through. The white garden of the sky
Is soundless. Her pale lips
Smile, gravely she sleeps: nothing moves, still he sips.

Awake, awake! Empty gardens sleep;
Dreaming the deep immaculate sky, they sleep,
Fade, vanish – not a shape
But fades, uncertain in that pure intensity.

Dream no more! Awake, lest, in your sleep,
Desire, oblivious, vanish where the deep,
Silent, immaculate sky
Will keep you sleeping, dreaming forever of sleep.

AN ANSWER

Most difficult and dear, here on my bed,
Your sorrow, more than your old fabled love,
Moves in me what remains for it to move
Of love and pity; and, uncomforted,
And frank as the assent it would inspire,
Tempts me to trust, once more, my own desire.

Though I have [illegible]ored and lie down to rest,
I cannot sleep, fearing that you might be
Nailed there awake and waiting on the tree.
But, if I doubt my doubt as self-possessed,
I cannot help but wonder whether shame
Or scorn or hurt murmurs your dreadful name.

I try by words to imitate your word,
Though I know that my speech, even if true,
Names only what is not the same as you;
And, as I must, I know my death conferred
On every flesh and see, revealed to sense,
The enormity of perfect difference.

I am my first and last, but, though, too late,
Dumb, blind, and certain, change will mend this dim
Unfaithful likeness of its antonym,
I cannot comfort you, if you should wait,
Passionate in your logical intent,
For me to know how else I dare assent.

A SONG FOR RISING

My life is mine to have well or to lose.
I struggle to conceive, not who I am,
But, in the constant end that I must choose,
The being that permits me to its sum.

Even by that attempt I must profane
The certain no pretense of mine can change,
From which each hopeful lie departs in vain.
I am the brief departure lies derange.

So here I am at last, and you are there,
The same as you have always been, the true,
The final and the necessary care.
All that I am and hope to be is you.

But why you are or why I am or why
I think to ask I will no longer guess.
The manifest dilemma that was I
Confronted you between its nothingness.

THE DREAM

I dreamed last night I dreamed, and in that sleep
You called me from the stair, as if the dead
Command each fragile sleeper to awake
And free them from their darkened wandering.
I knew that you would come into the room.
I waited for the sudden tug and slant
Upon the edge of my vague spectral bed.
I woke, looked at my watch, and sucked my breath.
There, in my stead, still waiting and still true,
Lay him who dreamed me still and, maybe, you.

THE CENTAUR OVERHEARD

Once I lived with my brothers, images
Of what we know best and can best become.
What I might be I learned to tell in eyes
Which loved me. Voices formed my name,

Taught me its sound, released me from its dread.
Now they are all gone. When I prance, the sound
From dark caves where my hooves disturb the dead
Orders no other promise. Underground,

Streams urge their careless motion into air.
I stand by springs to drink. Their brimming poise
Repeats the selfish hope of who comes there.
But I do not look, move, or make a noise.

AUTUMN SHADE

AUTUMN SHADE

1

The autumn shade is thin. Grey leaves lie faint
Where they will lie, and, where the thick green was,
Light stands up, like a presence, to the sky.
The trees seem merely shadows of its age.
From off the hill, I hear the logging crew,
The furious and indifferent saw, the slow
Response of heavy pine; and I recall
That goddesses have died when their trees died.
Often in summer, drinking from the spring,
I sensed in its cool breath and in its voice
A living form, darker than any shade
And without feature, passionate, yet chill
With lust to fix in ice the buoyant rim –
Ancient of days, the mother of us all.
Now, toward his destined passion there, the strong,
Vivid young man, reluctant, may return
From suffering in his own experience
To lie down in the darkness. In this time,
I stay in doors. I do my work. I sleep.
Each morning, when I wake, I assent to wake.
The shadow of my fist moves on this page,
Though, even now, in the wood, beneath a bank,
Coiled in the leaves and cooling rocks, the snake
Does as it must, and sinks into the cold.

2

Nights grow colder. The Hunter and the Bear
Follow their tranquil course outside my window.
I feel the gentian waiting in the wood,
Blossoms waxy and blue, and blue-green stems
Of the amaryllis waiting in the garden.
I know, as though I waited what they wait,
The cold that fastens ice about the root,
A heavenly form, the same in all its changes,
Inimitable, terrible, and still,
And beautiful as frost. Fire warms my room.
Its light declares my books and pictures. Gently,
A dead soprano sings Mozart and Bach.
I drink bourbon, then go to bed, and sleep
In the Promethean heat of summer's essence.

3

Awakened by some fear, I watch the sky.
Compelled as though by purposes they know,
The stars, in their blue distance, still affirm
The bond of heaven and earth, the ancient way.
This old assurance haunts small creatures, dazed
In icy mud, though cold may freeze them there
And leave them as they are all summer long.
I cannot sleep. Passion and consequence,
The brutal given, and all I have desired
Evade me, and the lucid majesty
That warmed the dull barbarian to life.
So I lie here, left with self-consciousness,
Enemy whom I love but whom his change
And his forgetfulness again compel,
Impassioned, toward my lost indifference,
Faithful, but to an absence. Who shares my bed?
Who lies beside me, certain of his waking,
Led sleeping, by his own dream, to the day?

4

If I ask you, angel, will you come and lead
This ache to speech, or carry me, like a child,
To riot? Ever young, you come of age
Remote, a pledge of distances, this pang
I notice at dusk, watching you subside
From tree-tops and from fields. Mysterious self,
Image of the fabulous alien,
Even in sleep you summon me, even there,
When, under his native tree, Odysseus hears
His own incredible past and future, whispered
By wisdom, but by wisdom in disguise.

5

Thinking of a bravura deed, a place
Sacred to a divinity, an old
Verse that seems new, I postulate a man
Mastered by his own image of himself.
Who is it says, *I am?* Sensuous angel,
Vessel of nerve and blood, the impoverished heir
Of an awareness other than his own?
Not these, but one to come? For there he is,
In a steel helmet, raging, fearing his death,
Carrying bread and water to a quiet,
Placing ten sounds together in one sound:
Confirming his election, or merely still,
Sleeping, or in a colloquy with the sun.

6

Snow and then rain. The roads are wet. A car
Slips and strains in the mire, and I remember
Driving in France: weapons-carriers and jeeps;
Our clothes and bodies stiffened by mud; our minds
Diverted from fear. We labor. Overhead,
A plane, Berlin or Frankfurt, now New York.
The car pulls clear. My neighbor smiles. He is old.
Was this our wisdom, simply, in a chance,
In danger, to be mastered by a task,
Like groping round a chair, through a door, to bed?

7

A dormant season, and, under the dripping tree,
Not sovereign, ordering nothing, letting the past
Do with me as it will, I savor place
And weather, air and sun. Though Hercules
Confronts his nature in his deed, repeats
His purposes, and is his will, intact,
Magnificent, and memorable, I try
The simplest forms of our old poverty.
I seek no end appointed in my absence
Beyond the silence I already share.

8

I drive home with the books that I will read.
The streets are harsh with traffic. Where I once
Played as a boy amid old stands of pine,
Row after row of houses. Lined by the new
Debris of wealth and power, the broken road.
Then miles of red clay bank and frugal ground.
At last, in the minor hills, my father's place,
Where I can find my way as in a thought –
Gardens, the trees we planted, all we share.
A Cherokee trail runs north to summer hunting.
I see it, when I look up from the page.

9

In nameless warmth, sun light in every corner,
Bending my body over my glowing book,
I share the room. Is it with a voice or touch
Or look, as of an absence, learned by love,
Now, merely mine? Annunciation, specter
Of the worn out, lost, or broken, telling what future,
What vivid loss to come, you change the room
And him who reads here. Restless, he will stir,
Look round, and see the room renewed, and line,
Color, and shape as, in desire, they are,
Not shadows but substantial light, explicit,
Bright as glass, inexhaustible, and true.

10

My shadow moves, until, at noon, I stand
Within its seal, as in the finished past.
But in the place where effect and cause are joined,
In the warmth or cold of my remembering,
Of love, of partial freedom, the time to be
Trembles and glitters again in windy light.
For nothing is disposed. The slow soft wind
Tilting the blood-root keeps its gentle edge.
The intimate cry, both sinister and tender,
Once heard, is heard confined in its reserve.
My image of myself, apart, informed
By many deaths, resists me, and I stay
Almost as I have been, intact, aware,
Alive, though proud and cautious, even afraid.

NEW POEMS

LIVING TOGETHER

Of you I have no memory, keep no promise.
But, as I read, drink, wait, and watch the surf,
Faithful, almost forgotten, your demand
Becomes all others, and this loneliness
The need that is your presence. In the dark,
Beneath the lamp, attentive, like a sound
I listen for, you draw near – closer, surer
Than speech, or sight, or love, or love returned.

WANDERING

1

Customs, but there seems nothing to declare.
My own illusion, and taking my own dare,

alone, I wait the likeness of the need
my loneliness will teach me, not a creed

or history, but a fable, dangerous
as pure occasion, as ambiguous.

Forty years young! The spectral avatar
I wander toward will seem familiar, far

in future pasts, when I, with old defense,
dignify it in private consequence.

2

Dark rain, stone streets, and, on dim buildings, light
torpid and cold. In the bar, the erudite

antagonist defines the risk, the quest.
But who and what is he? The quiet man, dressed

in black, leaning in his chair, a cigarette
caught in his smile? old unappeased regret?

the promised other? or the friendly whore,
an image of my death, solicitor

beckoning toward the hyperbolic kiss,
who takes my fear, my hope, my trust for bliss,

and leaves me lonelier on the lonely bed?
Without direction, I confront the dead,

but not for mere adventure, not for spite.
I look toward someone in this cold, this night.

3

We kiss, and then I fill my time alone.
Nothing I think protects me; I atone

for some mistake, some truth, some ignorance
of carelessness, self-love, or innocence.

That knowledge will outlast this lust. But here,
now, undismayed by vanity and fear,

I know you walk the Luxembourg, afraid
of love, except the casual or the paid,

and know we feel the same deliberate end.
It brings you back, my enemy, my friend,

an end aloof and cruel, but profound,
other than love, a limit and a ground.

4

Another pick-up. Professionally kind,
but ruthless, a youthful body in a mind

without illusion, true, but merely true,
this is the brute appearance I live through.

Oh age and act of reason, comic mime,
clear as a theorem, chaste as space and time!

And we two? dreams of affection, unimpaired
exclusions of a faith unnamed, unshared.

5

Too much. I have the flu. I write my name
illegibly on checks, ironic claim

on what I am and have from my true past,
what I depend on, well or ill, the last

residue of decision, paid and sure.
Waking from a delirium, a pure

self which suffers the dream of happiness,
I lie content. For, after all, duress

is coffee, and a croissant, and a word
from strangers, human, comforting, absurd.

INSOMNIA

He wakes at four, and knows what he must do.
His book awaits him. Mercury and Saturn
Control the shadow cast by earth on day.
The surf is like a shadow on the moon,
His listening like a prayer, and his awareness
A pool, on which a mythic self appears.
Then, having thought aloud what might have been
For him who is the only one he knows,
In the pure present, in the light, he sleeps,
And wakens in the need to have no need.

CHORUS FOR THE UNTENURED PERSONNEL

If we are on probation, what's our crime?
Original sin, mysterious want of grace,
The apple that we ate in a happier time
Of learning, friendship, courtesy, and wit –
Our innocence! For see, the gorgon's face,
The discipline of hatred, our true text.
We read, in darkness visible, the X.

The relative is absolute, and judgment
Genius, and the point of stasis, where
You say it is. O mind beyond compare,
In what doubt, or in what impersonal
Intention, even tentative and small,
Shall you perceive an other than your will?

AN ELEGY: DECEMBER, 1970

Almost four years, and, though I merely guess
What happened, I can feel the minutes' rush
Settle like snow upon the breathless bed –
And we who loved you, elsewhere, ignorant.
From my deck, in the sun, I watch boys ride
Complexities of wind and wet and wave:
Pale shadows, poised a moment on the light's
Archaic and divine indifference.

This book was designed by Jaggard Blount. The type is Garamond, set by Atlantic Typographers; the paper is Mohawk Vellum; the binding is by Haddon Craftsmen. The jacket illustration was cut in wood by Barbara Scott.

PS3552 0872 L5
+Living together; +Bowers, Edgar
0 00 02 0208067 7
MIDDLEBURY COLLEGE